THE **OFFICIAL**
HEART OF MIDLOTHIAN
FOOTBALL CLUB ANNUAL 2013

Written by Paul Kiddie
Designed by Brian Thomson

A Grange Publication

© 2012. Published by Grange Communications Ltd., Edinburgh, under licence from Heart of Midlothian Football Club plc. Printed in the EU.

Photographs © SNS Group

ISBN 978-1-908925-06-0

£7.99

Contents

Manager's Welcome 06

Club Stats 08

Roll of Honour 09

The Road to Hampden 10

QUIZ: Spot the Ball 23

Jamie MacDonald 24

QUIZ: Denis' Maze 28

Derby Pix! 30

QUIZ: Cup Final Quiz 33

Waiting Game: Denis Prychynenko 34

Dream Debut: Fraser Mullen 36

QUIZ: Word Search 38

Out to Impress: Jamie Hamill 40

QUIZ: Guess Who? 43

Ones to Watch! 44

Contalmaison 46

Cups of Cheer! 48

QUIZ: General Knowledge 53

Hampden Memories 54

The BIG Question with Danny Grainger ... 58

Quiz Answers 60

Welcome

The official 2013 Heart of Midlothian annual is always popular with supporters and it gives me great pleasure as manager of this great club to introduce for the first time this year's edition, which I'm sure will once again prove another great read for all Jambos.

Packed full of exclusive interviews and interesting features with first team stars, there is something for everybody.

There is a look back on the fantastic William Hill Scottish Cup victory over Hibs at Hampden Park in May and the spotlight is also turned on three members of the triumphant squad – Jamie MacDonald, Danny Grainger and Denis Prychynenko.

Up-and-coming Fraser Mullen reflects on his memorable top team debut last season while a number of the club's most promising young stars are featured in the Ones To Watch – a section which will be more relevant than ever with the direction now being pursued by Hearts.

It's been a tough few months for Jamie Hamill as he battled back from a serious knee injury and I'm sure the fans will enjoy reading his reflections on his long journey back to fitness.

There's also a fascinating feature on Contalmaison, the French village where the opening day of the Battle of the Somme in World War One claimed the lives of fearless Hearts players who had signed up for McCrae's Battalion.

Of course, it wouldn't be the annual without quizzes to test your knowledge on Hearts and we have a few brain-teasers to get you thinking – even Lockie struggled on a couple!

From front to back, the 2013 annual is a winner.

Enjoy!

John McGlynn

Manager.

CLUB STATS

Formed:	*1874*
Champions:	*1895, 1897, 1958, 1960*
Scottish Cup:	*1891, 1896, 1901, 1906, 1956, 1998, 2006, 2012*
League Cup:	*1954-55, 1958-59, 1959-60, 1962-63*
1st Division Champions:	*1980*
Record Victory:	*21-0 v Anchor, EFA Cup, 30.10.1880*
Most Caps:	*Steven Pressley, 32 For Scotland*
Most League Appearances:	*Gary Mackay, 515 (1980-97)*
Most League Goals:	*John Robertson, 214 (1983-98)*
Most League Goals:	*Barney Battles*
	In A Season: 44 (1930-31)
Official Website:	*www.heartsfc.co.uk*
Official Mobile Site:	*heartsfc.wap.com*
Official Store:	*www.heartsdirect.co.uk*
Official Online TV Channel:	*HeartsTV*

THE HEART AND SOUL OF EDINBURGH...

ROLL OF HONOUR

Scottish Champions:	1894-95; 1896-97; 1957-58; 1959-60
Runners-Up:	1893-94; 1898-99; 1903-04; 1905-06; 1914-15; 1937-38; 1953-57; 1958-59; 1964-65; 1985-86; 1987-88; 1991-92; 2005-06
Scottish First Division Champions:	1979-80
Scottish FA Cup Winners:	1890-91; 1895-96; 1900-01; 1905-06; 1955-56; 1997-98; 2005-06; 2011-12
Scottish FA Cup Finalists:	1902-03; 1906-07; 1967-68; 1975-76; 1985-86; 1995-96
Scottish League Winners:	1954-55; 1958-59; 1959-60; 1962-63
Scottish League Cup Finalists:	1961-62; 1996-97
Victory Cup Finalists:	1918-19
Scottish League East & North Division Runners-Up:	1939-40
Scottish Southern League Cup Finalists:	1940-41
Texaco Cup Finalists:	1970-71

THE ROAD TO HAMPDEN

January 7, 2012 • *William Hill Scottish Cup* • *4th Round*
Hearts 1, Auchinleck Talbot 0 • *Scorers: Smith (83)*

Hearts were forced to battle hard to overcome a stuffy Auchinleck Talbot side who did the Junior game proud with a stuffy performance in their fourth-round meeting at Tynecastle.

As expected, the home side had the majority of the game but found it very difficult to breach the Ayrshire outfit's resolute back line, the outstanding performer being Talbot keeper Andy Leishman with a series of high-class saves.

Debutant Fraser Mullen scorned a golden opportunity to break the deadlock when he missed a first half penalty, Leishman throwing himself full stretch to keep the effort out.

Just as the tie appeared to be drifitng towards a replay, the hosts finally managed to get the goal they had been craving.

A long ball into the Talbot box caused a mix-up between Leishman and his defender which saw the ball spill out to the 20-yard mark where Gordon Smith was on hand to confidently steer a low drive Into the empty net.

The relief around the stadium was almost tangible, although Auchinleck were only denied a dramatic injury-time equaliser by an assistant referee's flag for offside after Pope had netted past MacDonald.

THE ROAD TO HAMPDEN

Hearts: MacDonald; Grainger (Morton 45); Webster; Barr (Glen 70); Mullen; Driver; Black; Robinson; Skácel; Novikovas (Templeton 45); Smith. Subs not used: Ridgers, Obua.

Auchinleck: Leishman; McGoldrick; Pope; Pettigrew; Robb; White (Park 78); Young; Faulds (Slavin 71); Milliken (McCann 45); Spence; Latta. Subs not used: McGarrity, Gillies.

Referee: John Beaton.

11

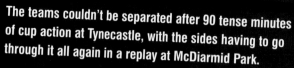

The teams couldn't be separated after 90 tense minutes of cup action at Tynecastle, with the sides having to go through it all again in a replay at McDiarmid Park.

The early goal the hosts had been hoping for duly arrived via the boot of David Templeton, the winger netting a fine solo effort with 10 minutes on the clock.

Scott Robinson had a great opportunity to double the advantage as half time approached but was denied by Peter Enckelman.

Saints were much more of a threat after the break and Francisco Sandaza had a header come crashing back off the bar as Steve Lomas' side attempted to get back into the fifth-round tie.

THE ROAD TO HAMPDEN

With 17 minutes remaining that challenge grew even more difficult, Dave Mackay receiving his marching orders for a second yellow card.

If Hearts thought the dismissal would help them see out the game, Saints had other ideas. Sandaza was thwarted by Jamie MacDonald when clean through on the keeper, but the equaliser arrived moments later when Cillian Sheridan beat the offside trap to slot home and set up a rematch on St Valentine's Day in Perth.

Hearts: MacDonald; Hamill; Webster; Zaliukas; McGowan; Black; Mrowiec; Robinson; Skácel (Taouil 76); Templeton (Driver 89); Elliott. Subs not used: Ridgers, Barr, Glen.

St. Johnstone: Enckelman; Mackay; Anderson; McCracken; C.Davidson; Croft (Keatings 83); Morris; M. Davidson (Millar 77); Robertson (Sheridan 45); Craig; Sandaza. Subs not used: Mannus, Oyenuga.

Referee: Craig Thomson.

Never-say-die Hearts kept alive their Scottish Cup dream with a stunning fightback against St Johnstone at McDiarmid Park.

Having forced a replay with a late goal at Tynecastle, Saints were given a taste of their own medicine as the Edinburgh club secured a quarter-final berth in the most dramatic of circumstances.

Murray Davidson looked to have won it for the home side when he found the top corner with just seven minutes remaining.

However, as the seconds ticked away Suso was brought down in the box by former Jambo Alan Maybury. Jamie Hamill kept his nerve to convert with what was practically the last kick of normal time.

There were chances at both ends during extra time, but the one that counted fell to captain Marius Zaliukas. He was the first to react after the ball came back off the bar into a crowded penalty area, the Lithuanian international smacking a shot into the back of the net to send the visiting fans wild with delight.

St. Johnstone: Mannus; Anderson (Oyenuga 106); Maybury (Haber 93); Morris; Wright; McCracken; Millar (Croft 70); Davidson; Sheridan; Craig. Subs not used: Enckelman, Keatings.

Hearts: MacDonald; Hamill; Webster; Zaliukas; Grainger (McGowan 74); Mrowiec; Robinson; Taouil (Suso 80); Obua (Templeton 65); Skácel; Elliott. Subs not used: Ridgers, Smith.

Referee: Brian Winter.

THE ROAD TO HAMPDEN

15

Another home tie resulted in another replay after Hearts and St Mirren shared four goals in an entertaining Tynecastle encounter.

The Buddies stunned their hosts by taking the lead in the first half, Graham Carey blasting home a superb 20-yard free kick.

Recent signing Craig Beattie then notched his first goal for Hearts, levelling things 10 minutes later when he headed home Danny Grainger's cross at the back post.

Beattie then turned provider shortly after the break to set up substitute Rudi Skácel for yet another strike against the team from Paisley,

and it seemed as if Hearts were on course for a semi-final meeting with Celtic at Hampden Park.

But three minutes from time, the home fans were silenced as Saints burst forward to snatch an equaliser. Gary Teale forced a terrific stop from Jamie MacDonald but Nigel Hasselbaink was on hand to steer home the rebound with the aid of a slight deflection off Marius Zaliukas.

Hearts: MacDonald; McGowan; Zaliukas; Webster; Grainger; Taouil; Black; Mrowiec (Skácel 37); Driver; Elliott; Beattie. Subs not used: Ridgers, Barr, Glen, Morton.

St. Mirren: Samson; Van Zanten; Mair; Goodwin; Carey; McGowan; Thomson; McLean (Murray 56); Teale; Hasselbaink; Thompson. Subs not used: Smith, McAusland, Mooy, Barron.

Referee: Stevie O'Reilly.

THE ROAD TO HAMPDEN

St Mirren: Samson; van Zanten; McAusland; Mair, Carey; Teale (Mooy 79); Goodwin; Murray (Tesselaar 69); Thomson; Thompson; Hasselbaink. Subs not used: Smith, McGregor, Barron.

Hearts: MacDonald; McGowan; Webster; Zaliukas; Grainger; Hamill; Barr; Black (Robinson 90); Driver; Skácel (Suso 88); Beattie (Glen 90). Subs not used: Ridgers, Novikovas.

Referee: Stevie O'Reilly.

Hearts made no mistake at the second time of asking as they comfortably saw off the challenge of St Mirren in Paisley to set up a semi-final meeting against Celtic at Hampden Park.

Goalkeeper Jamie MacDonald was the hero for the visitors after keeping the scoresheet blank with a superb first-half penalty save from Graham Carey, Marius Zaliukas having been penalised for handball.

The Edinburgh club made the most of the reprieve, Jamie Hamill sending an unstoppable 25-yarder soaring past Craig Samson to send the visitors in at the break in bouyant mood.

Both teams struggled to find any sort of fluency after the interval, and it was left to the scourge of St Mirren, Rudi Skácel, to continue his remarkable scoring record against them to make the tie safe.

Andrew Driver was the provider as he picked out the Czech ace seven yards out, and the prolific midfielder measured his shot before sliding the ball past Samson.

17

Hearts set up the first all-Edinburgh Scottish Cup Final in living memory with a controversial victory over Celtic at Hampden Park.

After a goalless opening 45 minutes, midfield talisman Rudi Skácel pounced two minutes after the restart to hand the initiative to the Jambos.

Crucially, Craig Beattie had been introduced for Scott Robinson during the interval, and the former Celt was involved in the build-up to the opener with his pass being deflected off Kelvin Wilson into the path of the Czech star who kept his composure after rounding Fraser Forster to smash an angled left-foot shot into the net.

The Tynecastle side rode their luck at times with Celtic hitting the woodwork twice, and they were left reeling when Gary Hooper headed home from a suspicious-looking offside position with just three minutes remaining.

Heads refused to go down, however, and in a dramatic finale, Hearts were awarded a penalty kick in injury time after referee Euan Norris spotted a handball in the box as Marius Zaliukas fired in a shot at goal.

Once the Celtic protests had finally calmed down, Beattie stepped up to score one of the most important goals of his career - and famously celebrated by ripping his top off and sprinting round the track at the back of the goal, pursued in vain by a clutch of team-mates!

There was still time for Celtic to voice their own claims for a spot kick for a handball against Andy Webster, but TV replays showed the referee called it correctly, and Hearts were soon dreaming of more Scottish Cup Final glory, this time against their city rivals.

THE ROAD TO HAMPDEN

Hearts were crowned William Hill Scottish Cup champions after demolishing city rivals Hibs 5-1 at Hampden Park in what will go down as the club's biggest cup victory in history.

Darren Barr got the Maroons' party started on 12 minutes with his first goal for Hearts, before Rudi Skácel's deflected shot to put the Gorgie side two up inside 20 minutes, only for James McPake to pull one back shortly before half time to give the Easter Road outfit renewed hope.

However, any aspirations of a comeback were snuffed out just moments into the second period when Pa Kujabi hauled Suso down inside the box, Danny Grainger converting the spot kick.

The Hibs defender was red-carded for the infringement and with his dismissal went his team's chances of ending their long wait for Scottish Cup glory.

Ryan McGowan's diving header made it four minutes later, before Czech ace Skácel grabbed his second with 75 minutes on the clock.

THE ROAD TO HAMPDEN

Hearts: MacDonald; McGowan; Webster; Zaliukas; Grainger; Suso (Beattie, 76); Barr; Black (Robinson, 86); Driver (Taouil, 84); Skácel; Elliott. Subs not used: Ridgers, Prychynenko.

Hibs: Brown; Doherty; McPake; Hanlon; Kujabi; Claros (Sproule, 42); Osborne; Stevenson; Soares (Francomb, 76); O'Connor (Doyle, 54); Griffiths. Subs not used: Grant, O'Hanlon.

Referee: Craig Thomson

ANDREW DRIVER

SPOT THE BALL!

Can you work out which one is the real ball in the picture below?

Answers on Pages 60 & 61

JAMIE MacDONALD

TOP OF THE TREE

*Keeper **JAMIE MacDONALD** achieves ambition by getting his hands on No. 1 jersey.*

It has been a long and difficult climb, but Hearts goalkeeper Jamie MacDonald has eventually reached the top of the tree.

A decade after turning full-time with the Edinburgh club, the Gorgie star can finally claim to be Jambos' No.1.

After spending years as an understudy to the likes of Craig Gordon and Steve Banks, the Broxburn ace was delighted to see the coveted digit emblazoned on his strip.

"It has been a very long time trying to get to this stage," he said. *"It's quite a nice feeling to actually have the No. 1 on the jersey, even though I played quite a few times last season.*

"The kit man told me it was there if I had wanted it. I think I had said previously I'd maybe keep the No. 30 as I'd had it for the past six or seven years and had become quite attached to it. But I couldn't turn down the opportunity to have No.1 as it's not often in your career you get that chance. In goalie terms, it means a lot.

"It's been 10 years full-time here so it's been a long road, but I've eventually managed to get to the top of the tree, if you want to call it that."

Having benefited from the stars who kept him out of the starting XI, MacDonald is hoping he can now pass on some words of advice to the stars of the future such as Scotland U21 shot-stopper Mark Ridgers and Jack Hamilton.

He said: *"I maybe didn't have as many chances as I'd have liked in the past, but the people in front of me have always been top quality performers such as Antti Niemi - it was a dream to come to a club and train with a top internationalist like him.*

"Then Craig Gordon started to break through and look what he's gone on to achieve. Steve Banks was fantastic as well, and more recently Marian Kello, so I have been very fortunate to work with people like that.

"I'd like to think I can help the likes of Mark Ridgers and Jack Hamilton to kick on with my experience. I have been fortunate to have played in some very big games such as two Scottish Cup Finals.

"Hopefully we can keep producing young keepers, and especially young Scottish boys. Mark is a fantastic keeper and Jack has loads of potential.

SCOTT ROBINSON

CALLUM PATERSON

DENIS' MAZE

Denis has left his training bag at the centre of this maze.

Can you help him find it?

Answers on Pages 60 & 61

adidas

wonga.com

ARVYDAS NOVIKOVAS

DERBY PIX!

Hearts 2, Hibs 0
28 AUG 2011

WEBSTER, STEVENSON, JONSSON CELEBRATING

WEBSTER SCORING

STEVENSON SCORING

MROWIEC, MCGOWAN,
ELLIOTT, SKACEL, KELLO
& SUTTON CELEBRATING

SKACEL
SCORING

I'LL PAINT
THIS PLACE
MAROON

Hibs 1, Hearts 3
02 JAN 2012

BLACK'S
PAINT THIS PLACE
MAROON T-SHIRT!

31

Hearts 2, Hibs 0
18 MAR 2012

BEATTIE AND SKACEL CELEBRATING

SUSO SCORING

SUSO AND CROWD CELEBRATING

CUP FINAL QUIZ!

Test your memory of the victory over Hibs in the 2012 William Hill Scottish Cup Final with these ten questions.

1. Who scored Hearts' first goal in the 5-1 victory?

2. Who scored from the penalty spot?

3. Which Hibs player received two yellow cards?

4. Can you name the unused substitutes on the Hearts bench?

5. Rudi Skácel netted twice in the final to bring his season's total to how many?

6. Who refereed the 2012 William Hill Scottish Cup Final?

7. When was the last all-Edinburgh Scottish Cup Final?

8. True or False - Paulo Sergio used to manage Benfica before joining Hearts?

9. Who did Hearts defeat in the semi-final?

10. Fill in the missing name: Barr, Grainger, Skácel,and _____?

Answers on Pages 60 & 61

DENIS PRYCHYNENKO

WAITING GAME

*Patience pays off in style for Scottish Cup winner **DENIS PRYCHYNENKO.***

Delighted Denis Prychynenko won his game of patience in some style after waiting eight months for a taste of first-team action last season.

The towering midfielder made his first-team debut as a substitute in the 3-0 victory over Aberdeen at Tynecastle at the end of March, going on to make a further four appearances including an outing in the William Hill Scottish Cup semi-final triumph over Celtic at Hampden Park.

The German-born Ukrainian's form saw him retain his place in the cup final squad for the showdown against Hibs on May 19 and although his involvement was restricted to an unused replacement at the National Stadium, getting his hands on a coveted winner's medal completed a dream campaign for the young player who signed for the club from Tennis Borussia Berlin in June 2010.

"Yes, it was probably the best year of my life because I made my debut," he said.

"Even though I didn't play for the first eight months of the season, it was still the best year of my life. Just because of the debut, the final… it was a great experience.

"It was great to come on in the semi-final of the Scottish Cup for 15 minutes. I felt like a part of the team. We won the Scottish Cup, and although I didn't come on in the final I was still in the squad and felt part of the team, so I was very happy."

Having enjoyed the taste of the big time, the 20-year-old is eager to sample more top team action as the current campaign unfolds.

He said: *"If I play then I know it's because of me and I've worked hard in training. If I don't play, then I know I've done something wrong. So I hope I'm going the right way about it just now, and – fingers crossed – there are more exciting times ahead."*

And his aspirations for 2013?

"To be a regular in the first team and do as well as we can in the league," he said.

FRASER MULLEN

DREAM DEBUT

*Talented youngster **FRASER MULLEN** will long remember his first outing for Hearts.*

Regardless of what he goes on to achieve in his career, youngster Fraser Mullen is unlikely to forget the events of January 7, 2012.

The date will remain special for the full-back, who was handed his first-team debut in the William Hill Scottish Cup 4th round clash against Auchinleck Talbot.

A surprise starter for the Jambos as they embarked on what would ultimately prove to be a glorious road to Hampden Park, Mullen was the talk of the town after producing a man-of-the-match performance despite a first-half penalty miss.

"It was a big occasion and to make my debut in a famous competition like the Scottish Cup was very special," said the Gorgie ace, who has his cup-tie jersey framed in the house as a permanent reminder of his dream outing.

"The day before the game I was in the starting XI for the shaping of the team in training, so I had an idea at that stage that I would be in the team. I was told the good news the next day that I was definitely starting.

"I thought about the game a lot on the Friday but still managed to get a good night's sleep.

"The experience of being in the dressing room getting ready for the cup-tie was brilliant."

Most fans were surprised when he stepped up to take the spot kick, although he revealed it had all been planned beforehand.

"Before the game a few of the players told me that if we got a penalty, I could take it," he said. *"As things transpired we got one in the first half, but unfortunately I didn't manage to score it.*

"I had taken a few for the 19s so was quite confident, but it wasn't to be.

"It didn't prove too costly as we still managed to get through to the next round, and I was delighted to play my part in the victory."

Further opportunities last season proved hard to come by, but having signed a new one-year contract in the summer, Mullen is looking forward to adding to the experience.

He said: *"It was a great taste of first team action, and I want as much as I can get now. I was delighted to get a new contract at the end of the season, and I know it's up to me now to make the most of any opportunities which come my way."*

WORD SEARCH!

Can you find 10 words relating to the 2012 William Hill Scottish Cup Final in the grid below?

Find the words in the grid. Words can go horizontally, vertically and diagonally in all eight directions.

M	N	X	B	Y	Y	C	F	H	X	N
R	E	K	B	N	E	A	T	F	X	V
Z	D	B	T	D	N	N	R	N	K	Q
M	P	Y	A	S	K	A	C	E	L	G
R	M	R	Y	R	Y	P	F	G	P	R
F	A	K	H	B	R	R	G	K	E	A
P	H	M	P	M	Y	Q	O	V	R	I
N	A	W	O	G	C	M	I	L	T	N
M	C	R	R	K	X	F	D	Z	G	G
C	D	W	T	R	K	T	J	T	N	E
N	T	M	R	P	N	L	P	D	Q	R

BARR	FIVE	GRAINGER	MCGOWAN	SKACEL
FANS	GLORY	HAMPDEN	PARADE	TROPHY

Answers on Pages 60 & 61

38

DARREN BARR

JAMIE HAMILL

OUT TO IMPRESS

JAMIE HAMILL is aiming to put his injury nightmare behind him.

You suffered a nightmare injury before the William Hill Scottish Cup Final but can you select any high points of 2012?
Getting my holiday actually! Going away on the break was good after picking up the injury. Obviously the boys winning the Scottish Cup against Hibs was great as well - it was good to see a smile on everybody's faces at the end of a long season.

You obviously played a very important part in the success with your goal away to St Mirren in the William Hill Scottish Cup quarter-final replay.
Yeah, that's right. Obviously it's enjoyable to score a goal at any point, but it's obviously good during a cup run and especially with the boys going on to win it at Hampden Park. I'd obviously rather have been playing in the game, but it was just as good sitting on the sidelines. As I say, I wish I had played in it, but it's just one of those things which can happen in football.

How good an experience was the Sunday, the day after, and all the celebrations in Edinburgh?
It was good. I was a wee bit tender on the Sunday, though! It was just party on Saturday and Sunday and I really enjoyed it. But no, it was good to be part of. As I said it was great to see everybody happy and all the fans outside the stadium and all the way through the town following the bus. I think a few of the boys, the likes of Danny Grainger and Ryan McGowan, were partying for a week or two afterwards!

You were a dab-hand at the karaoke at the staff party on the Saturday night...
I can't remember that! That was me on medication... the beer medication... as I said, it was good. I enjoyed being in good company with all the boys and a good atmosphere. It would've obviously been a different story if we didn't win the cup. I don't think there would've been any party or any karaoke. But I think the next time we do it the karaoke will be banned for me!

In terms of 2013, I guess what you'll be looking forward to most is just getting fit, getting match fit and getting back into the team?
Yeah, that's right. Hopefully I can get back into the team on a regular basis and perform at a consistently high level and play my part. The boys did well last season, and it would be great if we could get another good run in the cup as well as the league.

You've got a new manager to impress. Is that a different kind of challenge when you've been out injured for so long?
Yeah, that's right, obviously it's difficult when you're injured as a player and there's a new manager who comes in when you're out of the team. My target, as I have said, is just to get back playing regularly after completing the rehab programme, and hopefully I'll be back to impress the new manager and we'll take things from there.

Jamie Hamill spoke to Phil Turnbull.

JOHN SUTTON

GUESS WHO?

Which Hearts player is holding the cup?

Answers on Pages 60 & 61

ONES TO WATCH...

BRAD McKAY

A ball-playing centre back who signed a new one-year contract in the summer. He's very aggressive in the air and is a great distributor of the ball from the back. Surging runs into the middle of the park are another trademark of the youngster. He links play well and is a leader and organiser, too. He's been with the club for a couple of years and has done excellently.

CALLUM TAPPING

Signed from Tottenham Hotspur and came into his own in the second half of last season. He sees a pass nice and early but can also get forward and score some important goals. He's got great energy and is a good box-to-box type of player.

SAM NICHOLSON

A quick and dynamic wide player, who is comfortable on either flank, Sam is technically very gifted. Needs to build his bulk up a bit more but can score goals. He's been at Tynecastle for five or six years and is somebody the club has high hopes for.

BILLY KING

A similar type of player to Sam except a little bit more direct. Has tremendous feet, is really quick and direct. He possesses a great shot and is another one the club is looking to develop into a top wide player or striker. Finished last season as the top scorer for the U19s and can play anywhere across the front.

IN HONOURED MEMORY OF THE PLAYERS, TICKET-HOLDERS AND SUPPORTERS OF HEART OF MIDLOTHIAN FOOTBALL CLUB WHO TOOK PART IN THE ADVANCE ON CONTALMAISON ON 1 JULY 1916.

*Come pack up your footballs and
scarves of maroon...
Leave all your sweethearts in Auld
Reekie toon.
Fall in wi' the lads for they're off
and away
To take on the bold Hun with old
Geordie McCrae*

REST IN PEACE, BOYS

CONTALMAISON

Since 2004, a handsome cairn in the French village of Contalmaison has become a special place for an ever-increasing number of visitors to the battlefields of the Great War (1914-18)

This cairn has huge significance for the Heart of Midlothian Football Club, as it was built in memory of the 16th (Service) Battalion of the Royal Scots which was raised in Edinburgh in November 1914, by the politician and businessman, Lieutenant Colonel Sir George McCrae.

At a critical time for the country, McCrae's Battalion of 1,350 officers and men was raised in record time, due in no small measure to 13 members of Hearts' playing squad who volunteered to join three of their colleagues who were already in service. After the Tynecastle men had led the way, the battalion soon had players from Raith Rovers, Falkirk and Dunfermline Athletic.

In addition, around 600 Hearts supporters followed the example of their heroes, and in turn, they were joined by those of the other clubs, including local rivals, Hibs.

Over the years, the Contalmaison cairn has been regularly enhanced by friends of McCrae's Battalion Trust, and today the flags of Scotland and France proudly fly on either side of a bench that was donated by The Willie Bauld Memorial Club.

The villagers of Contalmaison have also added a memorial to those local people who died in the Great War, and now the Trust has placed an impressive orientation stone on the site. This explains the position of the British and German armies on the infamous first day of the Battle of the Somme, an engagement that had a tragic impact on McCrae's Battalion, Heart of Midlothian Football Club and the village.

"IT IS A SPECIAL PLACE TO VISIT AND ANY SUPPORTERS IN THAT AREA OF FRANCE ARE ALWAYS WELCOME TO VISIT."

After a week-long artillery bombardment, on 1 July 1916, the British Army launched a massive assault on a 20-mile section of German positions to the north of the River Somme.

However, the big guns failed to destroy elaborate defences and German machine-gun fire, with artillery support, inflicted unimaginable slaughter on unprotected soldiers. In the blackest day in the history of the British Army, there were a staggering 57,470 casualties that resulted in 19,240 deaths.

Among the advancing troops was McCrae's which followed its sister battalion, the 15th Royal Scots, into the German gunfire on the right side of the main road from Albert to Bapaume. They broke through the German first line, but then faced heavily-defended fields in front of the fortified village of Contalmaison.

Small groups of British soldiers, including some from McCrae's Battalion, entered the village, and although they retreated after a counter-attack, it was the deepest penetration of the German positions on the first day of the battle.

However, there was no major breach of the German lines, and entire units of the British Army were wiped out in a matter of minutes. McCrae's suffered terrible losses, and at the end of the day, a unit of 21 officers and 793 men found that 12 officers and 624 men were missing.

Seven Hearts players died during the Great War, and three of these fine men were killed on the first day of the Battle of the Somme: Harry Wattie, Duncan Currie and Ernie Ellis. Later in the battle, a fourth Hearts player, Jimmy Boyd, was also killed, while several were wounded in the vicinity of Contalmaison, including Alfie Briggs and Pat Crossan.

The village was eventually taken by the British Army on 10 July 1916, but the Battle of the Somme raged until November 1916 and resulted in an horrendous 660,000 British and French casualties.

When the Great War finally ended in 1918, the damaged land, villages and towns were rebuilt, and the sacrifice of those who fought was remembered at impressive cemeteries and monuments along the Western Front.

One of these is the memorial to McCrae's Battalion which stands next to the rebuilt church in Contalmaison. Bronze plaques tell the story of the battalion and the contribution of the Heart of Midlothian Football Club.

It is a special place to visit, and any supporters in that area of France are always welcome.

DAVID SPEED

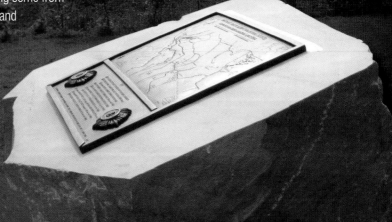

CUPS OF CHEER!

Hearts' victory over Hibs at Hampden Park in May 2012 secured win No. 8 in the Scottish Cup. Historian **DAVID SPEED** provides details of the club's seven other successes.

Standing: Joe Newton (Trainer), Jock Fairbairn, Jimmy Adams, and John MacPherson

Seated: Davie Russell, Isaac Begbie, Johnny Hill (Captain) and George Goodfellow

Front: Willie Taylor, Willie Mason, George Scott and Davie Baird

7th February, 1891
Heart of Midlothian 1 – Dumbarton 0
(Hampden: 12,000)

The attendance at Hearts' first Cup Final was remarkable considering that no Glasgow team was involved, and it included around 3,000 enthusiastic supporters from the Capital.

The game was played at the second Hampden Park (now Cathkin Park), and the crowd witnessed a tight and exciting contest that was decided by a goal after 15 minutes. The scorer was Willie Mason, signed from Wishaw Thistle, who ended a neat passing movement with a crisp low shot.

That season, Dumbarton shared the League Championship with Rangers, but they were unable to overcome Hearts' disciplined defence and were always vulnerable to the fast breaks of George Scott.

Hearts: Jock Fairbairn; Jimmy Adams and George Goodfellow; Isaac Begbie (Captain), John MacPherson and Johnny Hill; Willie Taylor, Willie Mason, Davie Russell, George Scott and Davie Baird.

Standing: Bob McLaren, Bob McCartney, Jock Fairbairn, Jimmy Mirk, Alex King and James Chapman (Trainer)

Seated: Davie Baird, Willie Michael, John Walker, George Hogg (Captain), Isaac Begbie and Davie Russell

14th March, 1896
Heart of Midlothian 3 – Hibernian 1
(Logie Green: 17,000)

This remains the only final to have been played outside of Glasgow, the game taking place at the ground of the old Edinburgh club, St Bernard's.

Hearts' players were well prepared and exploited Hibs' nervousness with a powerful start. A penalty for handball was given after only three minutes, and Davie Baird opened the scoring. In the second half, Alex King made it 2-0 from a tight angle, and then Willie Michael headed a third. John O'Neill scored Hibs' late consolation.

Hearts had won the League Championship in 1894-95, and the bulk of the Cup Final heroes would go on to win a further Championship medal in 1896-97.

Hearts: Jock Fairbairn; Bob McCartney and Jimmy Mirk; Isaac Begbie, Davie Russell and George Hogg (Captain): Bob McLaren, Davie Baird, Willie Michael, Alex King and John Walker.

6th April, 1901
Heart of Midlothian 4 – Celtic 3
(Ibrox: 16,000)

After a poor start to the season, the team was transformed with the signing of the St Bernard's pair Mark Bell and Bob Houston. With his brilliant dribbling and passing, Bobby Walker was then able to inspire a youthful side to a magnificent win in the Cup Final.

Some papers credited Walker with the opening goal and although he was involved, it was a blistering shot from Bill Porteous. William McOustra equalised, but Bell made it 2-1 for Hearts during a goalmouth scramble. In the second half, Charlie Thomson scored a third goal from a Walker pass, and then in a sensational contest, McOustra and Alex McMahon brought Celtic level.

However, after 80 minutes, when shots from Walker and Houston were blocked by the Celtic goalkeeper, a third attempt by Bell won this dramatic encounter.

Hearts: George Philip; Harry Allan and Davie Baird; George Key, Albert Buick, and George Hogg; Bill Porteous, Bobby Walker (Captain), Charlie Thomson, Bob Houston, and Mark Bell.

28th April, 1906
Heart of Midlothian 1 – Third Lanark 0
(Ibrox: 25,000)

Snow, hail and driving rain made things difficult for the players but Hearts, in a changed strip of light-blue, deserved to win.

After a spell of constant pressure, the deciding goal came with only nine minutes left. Bobby Walker tried to convert a George Couper cross, but after his effort was blocked, the ball broke to Hearts' strong and direct winger George Wilson, who rolled it into the net. The ex-Cowdenbeath attacker was obviously a hero with the fans. However, the man of the match was actually Hearts captain Charlie Thomson, who drove the team forward during the second period and started the passing move that ended with the winning goal.

Hearts: George Philip; Harry McNaught and David Philip; Frank McLaren, Charlie Thomson (Captain) and Jimmy Dickson; George Couper, Bobby Walker, Alex Menzies, David Wilson and George Wilson.

Standing: Donald McLeod (Asst. Trainer), Bobby Kirk, Davie Mackay, Tom Mackenzie, Tommy Walker (Manager), Willie Duff, Willie Bauld, John Cumming and John Harvey (Trainer)

Seated: Alex Young, Alfie Conn, Freddie Glidden, Jimmy Wardhaugh and Ian Crawford

16th May, 1998
Heart of Midlothian 2 – Rangers 1
(Celtic Park: 48,946)

Hearts made the best possible start and opened the scoring in the first minute. Steve Fulton was brought down in the box, and from the resulting penalty, Colin Cameron beat keeper Andy Goram with a low shot.

The game was then evenly fought, but after 52 minutes Stephane Adam controlled a long ball from Gilles Rousset and he sent it flying into the net with a right-foot drive from a tight angle. A goal from Ally McCoist brought Rangers back into the game with ten minutes left. However, the Hearts defence was magnificent, and the team withstood heavy pressure to ensure that a memorable victory was achieved.

Hearts: Gilles Rousset; Dave McPherson, David Weir, Paul Ritchie and Gary Naysmith; Thomas Flögel (Jim Hamilton), Stefano Salvatori, Steve Fulton (Captain) and Neil McCann; Stephane Adam and Colin Cameron. Also on the bench were John Robertson and Grant Murray.

21st April, 1956
Heart of Midlothian 3 – Celtic 1
(Hampden: 133,583)

With 60,000 tickets sold at Tynecastle, Hearts' greatest-ever support backed the team before the largest crowd ever to have watched the club.

After 20 minutes, Ian Crawford scored with a splendid 20-yard drive, and despite John Cumming's head injury, it became 2-0 just after half time. Alex Young headed the ball down to the feet of Crawford, and he quickly hooked it into the net. Celtic hit back in 55 minutes when the ball was forced over the line by Mike Haughney.

Nevertheless, Hearts regained their composure, and after 81 minutes victory was assured when Alfie Conn hit home a splendid shot from a headed pass by Willie Bauld.

Hearts: Willie Duff; Bobby Kirk and Tom Mackenzie; Davie Mackay, Freddie Glidden (Captain) and John Cumming; Alex Young, Alfie Conn, Willie Bauld, Jimmy Wardhaugh and Ian Crawford.

TENNENT'S LAGER   TENNENT'S LAGER

TENNENTS SCOTTISH CUP WINNERS 1997/98

13th May, 2006
Heart of Midlothian 1 – Gretna 1
Hearts won 4-2 on penalties
(Hampden: 51,232)

Hearts were well on top against the First Division side and eventually scored after 39 minutes. A long throw from Robbie Neilson caused chaos in the box, and Rudi Skácel smashed an angular shot into the net from six yards. Hearts' failure to take further chances was worrying, and after 76 minutes Gretna equalised. Ryan McGuffie steered the ball into the net after Craig Gordon had saved his initial penalty-kick.

Hearts spurned more chances throughout extra-time and had a big penalty shout refused when Skácel was fouled on the verge of netting the ball. Although Hearts' main penalty taker, Paul Hartley, had been sent off, overall class and composure won the shoot out. Pressley, Neilson and Skácel scored before Derek Townsley's kick was saved by Gordon. Michal Pospíšil scored, and when Gavin Skelton missed, Hearts had won the cup.

Hearts: Craig Gordon; Robbie Neilson, Steven Pressley, Ibrahim Tall and Panagiotis Fyssas; Deividas Cesnauskis (Saulius Mikoliunas), Paul Hartley, Bruno Aguiar (Julian Brellier), and Rudi Skácel; Roman Bednár (Michal Pospišil) and Edgaras Jankauskas. Also on the bench were Steve Banks and Christophe Berra.

GENERAL KNOWLEDGE

Test your knowledge on Hearts with the following ten brain teasers!

1. In what year was Heart of Midlothian FC founded?

2. From what club did John McGlynn arrive as manager in the summer of 2012?

3. Who did Hearts play in their opening league game of the 2012-13 Clydesdale Bank Premier League season?

4. Hearts' glorious William Hill Scottish Cup run began against who last season?

5. How many times have Hearts won the League Cup?

6. Umbro have been replaced by who as Hearts' official kit supplier?

7. Edgaras Jankauskas won the Champions League with which team?

8. Which player holds the appearances record for Hearts?

9. What is the predominant colour of the Hearts away kit this season?

10. What nationality is Jamie Hamill?

Answers on Pages 60 & 61

HAMPDEN MEMORIES

the BIG
QUESTION *with* DANNY GRAINGER

What has been your biggest achievement in football?

That has got to the be the 2012 Scottish Cup Final. To beat our biggest rivals in the final was good, but to get on the scoresheet and win in the manner we did was fantastic for me. It's the best day in my career, and I don't think it will ever be beaten.

Your biggest achievement away from the game?

Settling down with my wife Heather and having my son Oliver - that was the proudest moment of my life. I just love spending time with him when I'm not at the club.

Who has had the biggest influence on your career?

My mum Hilary and my dad Les. They have travelled the country with me ever since I was a youth player in England. They have always been there for me and are always on the phone after games, win or lose.

Who is the biggest laugh in the dressing room?

That is probably Jamie Hamill. He's always messing about! He's had a tough time with injury, and we've all tried to get him through it. Despite everything, he still managed a bit of banter with the lads, which was great.

Who is the biggest moaner in the squad?

I'd have to say Webby and myself are the two biggest moaners. For me I'll say it's passion, for Webby it's just because he likes a good moan, so he gets my vote for that one!

Who has the biggest appetite?

Definitely Andrew Driver! We went to Nando's one day and he polished off a starter, ordered a platter for three and demolished that before picking at other people's food!

ANDREW DRIVER: *BIGGEST APPETITE!*

What's the biggest game you have played in?

After missing out on so many cup finals, I couldn't wait to get out there at Hampden Park on May 19th, and it was a day I'll never forget.

'Big head' would refer to which member of the squad?

I would have to say that honour has to go to either Darren Barr or John Sutton, who both have absolutely huge heads. It's an ongoing joke in the dressing room.

JAMIE HAMILL: *BIGGEST LAUGH!*

What has been your biggest embarrassment?

We were having a pre-match before a game against Kilmarnock and the boss was telling me he thought I was carrying a bit of timber around the stomach. Earlier I had been telling the boys how that week my dog had eaten a sandwich my wife had made for me. But after what the gaffer said, they told me to stop blaming the dog and that I had eaten it, so we all had a good laugh around the table.

Who has the biggest brain?

I'm going to say John Sutton as he seems a bit boring. I reckon he goes home to read a dictionary or watch Countdown! Him and Webby seem quite intelligent - then we have Ryan McGowan at the opposite end of the scale!!

JOHN SUTTON: *BIGGEST BRAIN, AND BIGGEST HEAD!!!*

QUIZ ANSWERS...

Spot The Ball! – Page 23

Denis' Maze – Page 28

Cup Final Quiz – Page 33

1. Darren Barr.
2. Danny Grainger.
3. Pa Kujabi.
4. Mark Ridgers, Denis Prychynenko.
5. 18.
6. Craig Thomson.
7. 1896.
8. False - Sporting Lisbon.
9. Celtic.
10. McGowan (all the goalscorers from the final).

Word Search! – Page 38

M	N	X	B	Y	Y	C	F	H	X	N
R	E	K	B	N	E	A	T	F	X	V
Z	D	B	T	D	N	N	R	N	K	Q
M	P	Y	A	S	K	A	C	E	L	G
R	M	R	Y	R	Y	P	F	G	P	R
F	A	K	H	B	R	R	G	K	E	A
P	H	M	P	M	Y	Q	O	V	R	I
N	A	W	O	G	C	M	I	L	T	N
M	C	R	R	K	X	F	D	Z	G	G
C	D	W	T	R	K	T	J	T	N	E
N	T	M	R	P	N	L	P	D	Q	R

Guess Who? – Page 43

Answer: Darren Barr

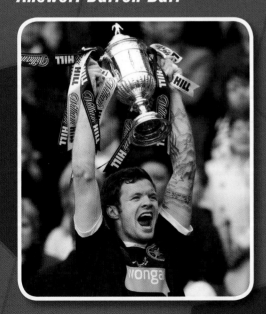

General Knowledge – Page 53

1. 1874.
2. Raith Rovers.
3. St Johnstone.
4. Auchinleck Talbot.
5. 4.
6. Adidas.
7. Porto.
8. Gary Mackay.
9. White.
10. Scottish.